OLD CARDONALD HAD A FARM

John A. Innes

GLASGOW CITY LIBRARIES

1993

BRITISH LIBRARY Cataloguing in Publication Data

Innes, John A
Old Cardonald Had a Farm
I. Title
941.443

ISBN 0-906169-38-0

Cover illustration: Cardonald Place Farm
Published by Glasgow City Libraries Publications Board
The Mitchell Library, North Street, Glasgow G3 7DN
Printed by Excel Print Services

ACKNOWLEDGEMENTS

Special thanks are due to two of the staff of Glasgow City Libraries, Elizabeth Carmichael, my editor, and Moira Thorburn, photographer.
Many other individuals and organisations have helped in the preparation of this book. I would like to thank them all, particularly for permission to reproduce the photographs on the pages indicated.

The Mitchell Library, back cover,pp4,5,10,12-17,32-38,52-56; Strathclyde Regional Archives,.pp39,45-50,58-59; Paisley Museum,p19; Cardonald Library; Paisley Abbey; Mr. Alexander Lochhead Jnr,.p60; Mr. G.T. Bell; Mr. W. Spalding,pp18,20,22-25,27-31,42-44; Mr. I. Stewart,p40; Mr. George Robin; Mr. F. Stone; Mr. R.J.S. Wiseman,p41; Duke of Hamilton Estate; Cardonald Parish Church,p21.

INTRODUCTION

Cardonald is just one of many suburbs of the city of Glasgow, but unlike Cathcart, Pollokshaws or Govan, it was never a burgh, or even a village, being part of Renfrewshire until incorporated into the city in 1926. Nevertheless Cardonald has a rich history, with its associations with the Royal House of Stewart, by way of Crookston Castle and Cardonald Place Farm.

Having been born and brought up in Cardonald, I have always had an interest in the area. Although I have lived at Kingsford, outside of Stewarton, since 1978, I have kept up my connections, through my friends in Cardonald and my long and continued association with the 30th Glasgow Scout Group.

I remember Cardonald, from my early childhood at the local school from 1929, when it was very much a rural area with a number of farms and open ground, where we played as children.

I have witnessed the steady urbanisation of Cardonald, over the years, with the building of the Western Heritable houses in the early 1930s, to the final build up, after World War II, when the remaining ground was acquired by Glasgow Corporation for house building.

Many districts of Glasgow have had local histories published, but apart from the Cardonald Parish Church centenary booklet, published in 1989 for private circulation, little has been written about Cardonald.

Cardonald Place Farm has recently been renovated by the current owner, after having lain derelict for many years. The building is now looking superb and the renovation does justice to the coat of arms of James Stewart of Cardonald which appears above the front entrance.

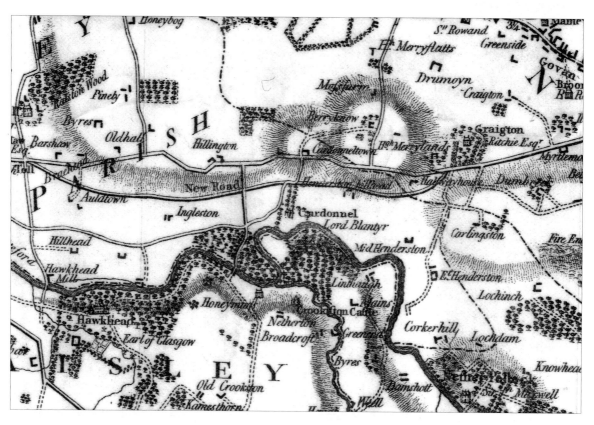

CARDONALD, FROM RICHARDSON'S MAP OF 1796, showing the old and new Paisley roads.

EARLY HISTORY

A plaque, displayed in the Abbey of Paisley, contains the origins of the Stewart dynasty. One of the Norman knights, who accompanied King David I on his return from England in the 12th century, was Walter Fitzalan. He was made High Steward of the Royal Household and the office became hereditary. Walter was given large tracts of land, in what is now Renfrewshire. The High Steward's coat of arms, which appears on the plaque is a blue and silver checked strip, on a gold background (called a fesse chequy), signifying the cloth on which the budget of Scotland was calculated.

This fesse chequy was to appear on many of the coats of arms of Stewarts, except the sovereigns, which was always a lion rampant. Walter gave some of his land to his knights, one of whom was Sir Robert de Croc, who was made responsible for the lands around the White Cart, from Cowglen to Hawkhead and outpost duty for the area from Renfrew Harbour to the Fereneze Gap. He used Kerr's Hill, now Hartlaw Crescent as his outlook. His land around the River Cart and Levern was known as "Crookisfeu".

About 1202, De Croc built a wooden motte on a drumlin, which is now occupied by Crookston Castle. Alexander, the fourth High Steward, is called Stewart, and was the founder of the two main branches of the Stewart family. His son, Sir John Stewart of Bonkyl was the ancestor of the Stewarts of Darnley, Alexander's grandson, Walter, the sixth High

PLAQUE IN PAISLEY ABBEY.

5

Steward, married Marjory Bruce, and their son became the first Stewart king, Robert II. Sir John's grandson, Sir Alexander Stewart of Darnley, lived at Darnley Castle, two miles south of Crookston.

The male De Croc line failed and Sir Alexander purchased Crookisfeu. It is understood that his grandson, Sir John Stewart of Darnley, built the stone castle at Crookston in 1413. It consisted of four corner towers, and a large vaulted main hall.

Having established himself at Crookston Castle, Sir John went to France in 1419, in command of the Scots Guards. His victory for the Dauphin, later King Charles VII of France, resulted in his elevation to Seigneur (Lord) d'Aubigny and he was given authority to quarter his Stewart fesse chequy with the Fleur de Lys of France.

Sir John was killed in 1429, at the Battle of the Herrings when he was assisting the Maid of Orleans. The present town hall in d'Aubigny near Orleans, was Chateau de Stuart, being their residence until 1672. Sir John had married Elizabeth, daughter of Duncan, the last Celtic Earl of Lennox. Their grandson, also Sir John, was created Lord Darnley in 1461 and so became the first Stewart Earl of Lennox.

In 1488 King James III was murdered by a group of nobles among whom were the Lennox-Stewarts. In retribution for this foul deed, his son King James IV laid seige to Crookston Castle employing the large cannon "Mons Meg", which had been hauled all the way from Edinburgh. The assault on the castle was only punitive, and most of the destruction was carried out by local men with picks and shovels. Crookston Castle remained habitable until 1506 when the Lennox Stewarts built a new palace at Inchinnan.

The castle continued to decay and the last known evidence of habitation was 1562, when it was inhabited by Charles 6th Earl of Lennox, brother of Lord Darnley, husband of Mary Queen of Scots.

STEWARTS OF CARDONALD

John, first Stewart Earl of Lennox had six sons, several of whom distinguished themselves with the Scots army in France. The sixth son Allan, of Cardonald, is most relevant to our story. In 1496 Isabella Norwell of Cardonald, was widowed by the death of her husband Sir William Stewart of Castlemilk. Their daughter Marion Stewart married Allan Stewart.

He became the first of the line of Cardonald Stewarts, which only survived for four generations (see chart on page 8).

Several authorities have questioned Allan Stewart's legitimacy. In the Register of the Great Seal of Scotland, his father refers to him as "Filius Carnalis" the translation of the Latin is open to question. It has also been stated that the bend dexter, in the first quadrant, a strip from top left to bottom right, on the coat of arms above the door of Cardonald Place Farm, refers to illegitimacy. This assumption is correct if the strip is black, as indicated on a number of Stewart crests eg. Earl of Moray, natural son of James V, but it is more likely to refer to the Stewarts of Minto whose fesse chequy coat of arms was surmounted by a red engrailed bend. The arms at Cardonald Place Farm were originally plain stone and only painted recently, with the bend dexter in black, which is probably incorrect. The crest also shows an escutcheon of red saltire with four roses, which refers to the Celtic Earls of Lennox, and completes the Lennox Stewart arms, and the lineage of the Cardonald Stewarts.

The Palace or place of Cardonald was probably built in 1565 the date shown on the crest, and was demolished in 1846, to be replaced by the current Cardonald Place Farm in 1848.

The second James Stewart of Cardonald and last of the male line is buried in Paisley Abbey and the gravestone set in the wall inside the Abbey has a description which as translated reads "Here Lies an Honorable man, James Stewart of Cardonald sometime Captain of the Guard of Scotland to France and deceased on 14th day of January 1584". The inscription surrounds the crest of the Darnley coat of arms. James died without issue and was survived by his three sisters, of whom Margaret married Sir John Stewart of Minto. As previously stated his coat of arms was a fesse chequy surmounted by red engrailed bend.

Crookston Castle had become derelict by the end of 17th century and the Cardonald male line of Stewarts had failed and the Minto Stewarts had married into the place of Cardonald. Sir John Stewart of Minto became Provost of Glasgow in the 1560s.

STEWARTS OF CARDONALD.

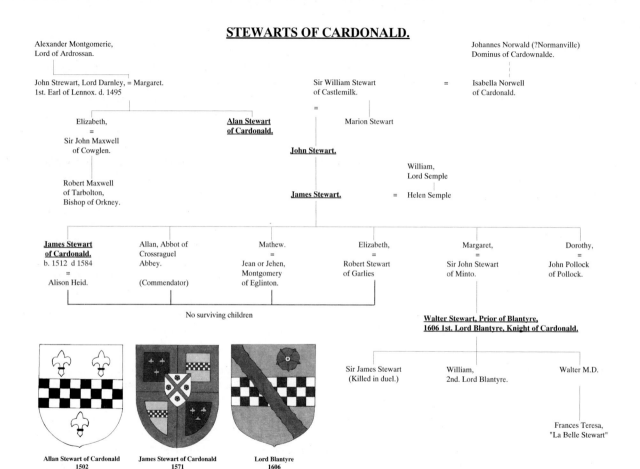

Alexander Montgomerie,
Lord of Ardrossan.

John Strewart, Lord Darnley, = Margaret.
1st. Earl of Lennox. d. 1495

Elizabeth,
=
Sir John Maxwell
of Cowglen.

Robert Maxwell
of Tarbolton,
Bishop of Orkney.

**Alan Stewart
of Cardonald.**

Sir William Stewart
of Castlemilk.
=

John Stewart.

James Stewart.

Johannes Norwald (?Normanville)
Dominus of Cardownalde.

Isabella Norwell
of Cardonald.
=

Marion Stewart

William,
Lord Semple

= Helen Semple

**James Stewart
of Cardonald.**
b. 1512 d 1584
=
Alison Heid.

Allan, Abbot of
Crossraguel
Abbey.

(Commendator)

Mathew.
=
Jean or Jehen,
Montgomery
of Eglinton.

Elizabeth,
=
Robert Stewart
of Garlies

Margaret,
=
Sir John Stewart
of Minto.

Dorothy,
=
John Pollock
of Pollock.

No surviving children

**Walter Stewart, Prior of Blantyre,
1606 1st. Lord Blantyre, Knight of Cardonald.**

Sir James Stewart
(Killed in duel.)

William,
2nd. Lord Blantyre.

Walter M.D.

Frances Teresa,
"La Belle Stewart"

Allan Stewart of Cardonald
1502

James Stewart of Cardonald
1571

Lord Blantyre
1606

8

BLANTYRE PERIOD

As the Reformation gained momentum after 1560, lay commendators were appointed to the reformed church in Scotland. Commendators had no particular religious purpose, but allowed those abbeys and priories a seat in the Scottish parliament. These positions were not always without hazard, as witness the fate of Alan, brother of James Stewart of Cardonald, who was roasted in oil, by the Earl of Cassillis to persuade him, then commendator of Crossraguel Abbey, to return the Abbey to the Kennedys, the Earl's family.

The posts of commendator tended to be handed out by King James VI to his friends, one of whom was Walter Stewart, only son of Sir John Stewart of Minto and Margaret Stewart of Cardonald. King James and Walter had been tutored by George Buchanan when they were children. In 1580 Walter was made commendator of Blantyre Priory. At that time the priory was a ruin and he used Cardonald as his base.

In 1587 Glasgow became a burgh of regality in the name of Walter Stewart of Cardonald. He held several high posts in Scotland becoming High Treasurer in 1596 and in 1606 was created Lord Blantyre.

When King James VI went to England after the Union of the Crowns in 1603, he claimed to rule Scotland by the pen, meaning that his orders would be put into effect by his childhood friend Walter, first Lord Blantyre.

The Blantyres remained at Cardonald for several generations and indeed many of the present day occupiers of Blantyre land pay feu duty to their lineal successor Sir David Baird. The last Lord Blantyre died in 1900 without issue.

18th CENTURY

This was the beginning of the Industrial Revolution in Britain when great changes were taking place in agriculture, industry and transport. At this time Cardonald consisted of Crookston Castle, by then a ruin and Cardonald House, with a number of small farms scattered throughout the area.

To the east was Pollok House, residence of the Maxwell family, while to the south west, was the estate of the Earls of Glasgow, who resided at Hawkhead House.

Crookston Castle was eventually acquired by the Duke of Montrose, who in turn sold it to the Maxwells of Pollok. In 1931 the castle became the first property of the National Trust for Scotland, since transferred to

Historic Scotland.

To the north was marshland between Govan and Renfrew, while to the south was Hurlet, where several mines existed. Near the River Levern were bleach fields and print fields, which polluted the rivers and had the effect of killing off the water mussels in the River Cart. These mussels produced top quality pearls, much sought after in world markets.

FOLK-LORE

Although strong connections exist between the Crookston/Cardonald area and Mary, Queen of Scots and her husband Henry, Lord Darnley, most of the tales relating to them are myths.

Sir Walter Scott was mistaken in writing that Mary observed the Battle of Langside from Crookston. She watched from Court Knowe, Cathcart.

It is the famous yew tree, with a trunk three metres in diameter, growing at Crookston Castle into the 19th century, which has caused most controversy.

a) It was widely believed that Mary and Henry plighted their troth beneath its branches. They never were at Crookston together.

CROOKSTON CASTLE FROM FOULIS ACADEMY ENGRAVING.

b) A set of coins minted 1565-6 to commemorate the marriage of Mary and Henry, called Mary Ryals but commonly referred to as "Crookston Dollars" had the "yew" tree on one side. This has been shown to be a palm tree.

   c) "Robt. Burns Ap. 4th 1777" on the yew trunk was shown not to have been carved by the bard, but by a local man of the same name.

All three items were meticulously researched and published by David Semple in "The Tree of Crookston" in 1876.

19TH CENTURY ONWARDS - RURAL TO URBAN COMMUNITY

The transformation from rural to urban community was largely caused by the coming of the railway and later tramways. The first railway to reach Cardonald was the Glasgow and Greenock Railway in 1841, though it was not until 1879 that a permanent station was built at Berryknowes Road bridge. The siting of this station influenced the building of Hillington Park Circus and other large houses in Berryknowes Road along with the houses in Kingsland and Queensland Drives.

The next important development was the building of the canal line and the opening of Crookston station in 1885. This encouraged the building of large villas in Ralston Avenue. The main spur to further development was the introduction of the electric tram from the Halfway to Paisley in 1903. From then on housebuilding gradually increased in Cardonald. The final upsurge in house building took place from 1931, when most of the existing farm land disappeared, with the building of the South Cardonald and Hillington houses. From 1935 Glasgow Corporation built a large number of houses to the west of Berryknowes Road.

After World War II, the remaining vacant land was purchased by Glasgow Corporation for the erection of prefabricated houses. These prefabs were ultimately replaced by flats and in some cases, tower blocks.

Thus Cardonald as we know it today is very much a built-up area, serving as a dormitory suburb of Glasgow.

MARYLAND HOUSE, BUILT 1707.

Apart from Rosshall House, Maryland is the only one of the estate houses still in existence in Cardonald. It stands west of Corkerhill Road, behind the current social security office, on the Paisley Road. Despite its name being suggestive of the American trade, there is no connection. The original name was believed to be High Merryland and it was the property of the Rowans of Govan and latterly the Stevens of Bellahouston. In 1902 the house was bought by the Archdiocese of Glasgow and used as a convent by the Sisters of Nazareth until Nazareth House was built. Today it is used as a private social club.

CRAIGTON HOUSE, BUILT 1740's.

Craigton Estate lay between what is now Barfillan Drive and Jura Street. The house and estate were owned by several merchant families - Ritchies, Dunlops and Hutchisons, all connected with the North American trade. Some of the buildings later housed the first Cardonald dog and cat home. Demolished 1920.

RALSTON HOUSE, BUILT 1797.

Ralston estate lay to the west of Crookston Road. The house was built for Mr. William Orr and later occupied by Mr. James Richardson (see Cardonald School, p23), and later still by the Cayser family, owners of the 'Clan Line' shipping company.

During the First World War the house was used as a military hospital and eventually became a residential home for invalided soldiers. In 1934 the estate was purchased by James Y. Keanie for the building of houses, and the mansion demolished. All that remains of the old estate are the two gatehouses on the Paisley Road and the stables, which are used by Ralston Golf Club.

ROSSHALL HOUSE, BUILT 1877.

To the south of Cardonald, off Crookston Road was the estate of Rosshall, originally owned by the Cowan family, who were involved in the building of the Paisley Canal Line for the Glasgow and South Western Railway. The estate passed in 1908 to the Lobnitz family, well known as dredger builders at Renfrew.

In 1948 Glasgow Corporation purchased the estate for £17,000, leasing the house to the Glasgow and West of Scotland Commercial College. The grounds became the responsibility of the Parks Department. In 1965 Rosshall Park was opened to the public. At the same time the college became part of Strathclyde University, and the house was used as the hotel and catering school. In 1982 the house was purchased by Glasgow Independent Hospitals Ltd and is now used as a private hospital.

ROSSHALL MAINS FARM.

This is the only farm still operating in the vicinity of Cardonald. It is situated on the south side of Scott's Road and takes in the land between the railway line and the White Cart. The farm has had two previous names, originally Old Mill Farm, then Hawkhead Mains. Other farms in the area were West Henderston Farm at the junction of Arbroath Avenue and Baldovie Road. The road up to the farm was what is now Selkirk Avenue. On the north side of Paisley Road was situated Hillhead Farm, at the top of Tweedsmuir Road and Wedderlea Drive. One of the last farms to disappear was South Hillington, situated at Kellhead Avenue. On the other side of the White Cart was Nether Crookston Farm, which ultimately succumbed to housing south of Brockburn Road.

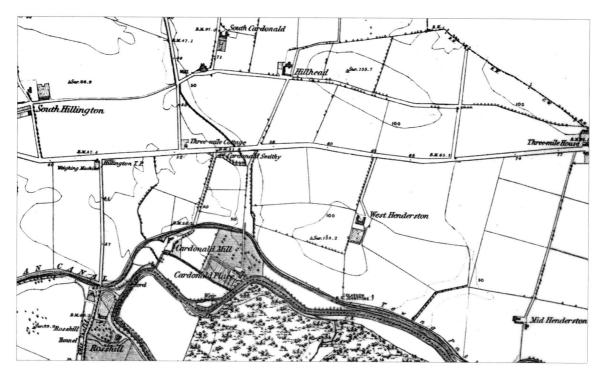

CARDONALD IN 1858 (Ordnance Survey).

CARDONALD MILL c1920.

From about 1789, a corn mill existed in Cardonald on a site now occupied by the Moulin Circus houses. In 1815 John Snodgrass, son of a Paisley mill owner, leased the mill from Lord Blantyre. The products from the mill were originally shipped through the nearby Paisley canal, and later by road. In 1848 the mill was largely rebuilt and remained in active use until 1958 when it was demolished along with adjoining cottages, to be replaced by the houses in Lade Terrace. The photograph is taken from the Old Mill Road with the mill in the background.

The Glasgow, Paisley and Ardrossan Canal was the brainchild of the 12th Earl of Eglinton, who promoted a scheme to link a new harbour at Ardrossan with Glasgow. Work began on the canal at Port Eglinton in 1807 and it reached Johnstone in 1810, when financial difficulties stopped any further extension. The canal passed through Cardonald at Corkerhill and proceeded west towards Cardonald Mill, then followed the long established Scott's Road to Hawkhead and thence to Paisley. The canal was 25 feet wide and 4 feet deep and so constructed as to avoid the need for any locks over its entire length. Passenger boats maintained a daily service between Glasgow and Paisley with various stopping places in Cardonald.

One of the original plans was to build a feeder canal from Nitshill to Crookston. This was abandoned in favour of a horse drawn railway which ran alongside Crookston Road. By 1868 the canal had lost most of its traffic to the railway and was finally purchased by the Glasgow and South Western Railway, who constructed a line from Shields Road junction to Paisley, following the line of the old canal.

The Old Toll House and Castle, Crookston Road.

THE OLD TOLL HOUSE ON CROOKSTON ROAD c1920.

This rural scene was taken from Crookston Road at the corner of what is now Brockburn Road and shows Crookston Castle, without any houses around it. From the house on the right, tolls were collected for using the road leading over to the Barrhead Road. Latterly this through road was abandoned and only gave access to Crookston Castle and Nether Crookston Farm.

CARDONALD PARISH CHURCH c1890.

Until 1887, there was no evidence of any church premises locally, except for a 12th century chapel, believed to be situated near Crookston Castle, at the side of the Brock Burn. Members and adherants of the Church of Scotland, in Cardonald, believed the time had come to have a church built. A committee, under the chairmanship of Mr. James Cowan of Rosshall, was set up to raise funds for the building of a church. The site chosen was at the corner of Cardonald Place Road and Paisley Road, which was approximately midway between Crookston and Cardonald railway stations and only a mile from the Halfway. The plot of ground was given by the land superior Lord Blantyre, at a nominal charge. The foundation stone was laid by Miss Cowan in May 1888, and the church was open for worship in February 1889. The photograph shows the church as originally built, without the two side extensions, which were added in 1899 and 1925. The large tree in the foreground, is roughly on the site of the Royal Bank of Scotland's Cardonald branch.

Three Mile House, Cardonald.

THREE MILE COTTAGE c1930.

As the name implies, the cottage was three miles from Paisley Cross, at the corner of Hillington Road and Paisley Road West. It is not known exactly when the cottage was built, but it is shown on the 1858 map. In recent times it became the property of Mr. J. MacDonald the local coal merchant, and was a popular stopping place for cyclists, where Mrs. MacDonald sold lemonade and confectionery. About 1932 the cottage was demolished to make way for the present shops. The view shows the cottage, with the fields in the background, now occupied by Keanie and Penilee houses, and South Hillington Farm on the left.

A school was started in Cardonald, at the Halfway, in 1790, by the local blacksmith, who taught a class in the rudiments of reading, writing and arithmetic. This voluntary teaching continued until 1826, when the school was put on a subscription basis. With the help of a £1000 legacy from Mr. J. Richardson of Ralston and contributions from local inhabitants a school and school house were built in 1860, on

Cardonald School.

CARDONALD SCHOOL c1920.

the present site. It is thought that the school was originally a single storey building, containing only two class rooms. Due to increase in the school population the school was extended in 1899 by the addition of a top storey. By 1911 further extensions were carried out with the addition of a central hall, and 4 more classrooms. About this time the schoolmaster Mr. Alexander Lochhead introduced a school uniform, incorporating a badge with the motto "Toujours Avant", based on the crest above the main door of Cardonald Place Farm. Cardonald School remained the only one in the district until the 1930s when Angus Oval and Hillington schools were built.

HALFWAY, LOOKING EAST, 1906.

Buchanan's Public House was demolished some years ago, to make way for a supermarket. The tramcar in the foreground has come from Paisley and is one of the original electric type. The only building still standing today is the tenement on the extreme right.

HALFWAY c1906.

This second photograph of the Halfway is taken from the same position as the previous view, and shows the original Halfway Post 0ffice and shops beyond, long since demolished. Howdens and Buchanans both opened at the Halfway in the 1890's. They were the only pubs in the area till, following a veto poll in the late 1950's, four other pubs appeared on the Paisley Road - the Parkway, Quo Vadis, Argosy and the Gaiety at the corner of Crookston Road.

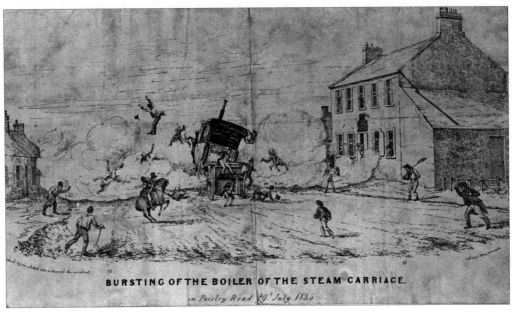

BURSTING OF THE BOILER OF THE STEAM CARRIAGE.

on Paisley Road 29.º July 1834

ACCIDENT AT THE HALFWAY.

In April 1834 steam carriages were introduced on the Paisley Road, operating from George Square in Glasgow, to the Tontine Hotel in Paisley. There were three carriages per day, in each direction, and the fare ranged from 6d to 1/6d, depending on where the passenger sat.

On 26th July 1834 a steam carriage stopped at the Halfway, and as the driver proceeded to start up the engine, a wheel came off. The resulting collapse of the carriage caused the boiler to blow up, killing five people and injuring many more. As a result of this disaster, the Court of Session banned the use of steam carriages in Scotland. It was reported that the cause of the accident was sabotage on the part of the road trustees.

Crookston Road.

CROOKSTON ROAD IN c1932.

The road has existed for more than two centuries, it is shown in the map of 1796. The road originally started at the Old Paisley Road and crossed the existing Paisley Road (laid out in 1753), in a southerly direction towards Scott's Road and Howford Bridge, over the White Cart and finally joined up with the Barrhead Road.

The shop on the right was built by Mr. Shaw, the builder of the adjacent bungalows and served, in its time, as a newsagent with a tea room and lending library. It is known that this site was at one time a toll house with a thriving restaurant and tea garden. Today it boasts a "fast food" shop.

PAISLEY ROAD WEST, LOOKING EAST, c1930.

Taken from the corner of Tweedsmuir Road. The only traffic on the road is two Midland buses, which operated between Glasgow and Ardrossan. The houses in the distance are those at Blairgowrie Road. Note the gas lights on the tram standards and the row of advertising hoardings along each side of the road.

PAISLEY ROAD WEST, LOOKING WEST, c1930.

The Paisley Road as we know it today was laid out as a toll road in 1753. The original road took a more northerly route. Starting at the Halfway, it crossed the front of the present Moss Heights, over Berryknowes Road towards Hillington Gardens, followed the lane between Wedderlea Drive and Invergyle Drive and then towards South Hillington Farm over Southwold Road, finishing at Barrshaw Park. This view looks from Cardonald Parish Church with Barr's garage and Post Office on the left, and MacDonald's Cafe and Paisley Provident shop on the right. In the distance is Three Mile Cottage with the trees of Ralston Estate beyond.

Midlothian & Lothian Gardens, Cardonald.

FIFE AVENUE COMPLEX, FROM WEDDERLEA DRIVE.

Taken before 1930 because from that date there were advertising hoardings along this stretch of the Paisley Road. The terraced houses were built in 1905 and although on the Paisley Road they were given the names Midlothian and Lothian Gardens, being divided by Fife Avenue. The terraced houses at the rear of the picture are those on Berwick Drive, previously known as Roxburgh Circus.

Lennox Road, Cardonald

LAMINGTON ROAD C1920.

After Cardonald became part of the City of Glasgow in 1926, many of the street names were changed to avoid duplication. Lennox Avenue became Lamington Road, Hillhead Road, named after the farm, became Tweedsmuir Road and Carlyle Drive became Traquair Drive. On the other side of the Paisley Road Mill Road became Moulin Road

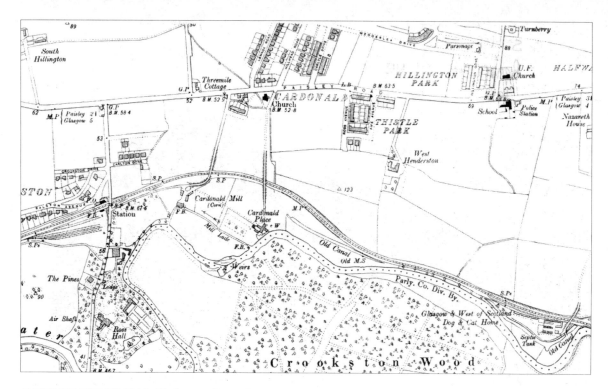

CARDONALD IN 1916, (Ordnance Survey).

NAZARETH HOUSE.

Nazareth House was built in 1906, in the grounds of the Maryland Estate, as a home for destitute children and aged poor, but nowadays geriatric patients are cared for by the Sisters.

CHURCH OF OUR LADY OF LOURDES.

At a census taken in 1887, there were believed to be only 15 residents of the Roman Catholic faith in the Cardonald district, and they came under the parish of St. Anthony's in Govan. Masses were first said in Cardonald in Maryland House and then from 1906 in the chapel of Nazareth House. A mission established in Cardonald used this chapel till, in 1922, a small church was built on what became Lourdes Avenue. By 1936, there was a need for a much larger church, and in May 1939, the church of Our Lady of Lourdes was opened. This view shows the imposing building in Lourdes Avenue.

CARDONALD STATION IN 1961.

The railway came to Cardonald as early as 1841 when the Glasgow and Greenock Railway was built. A station at the Berryknowes Road bridge, known as Moss Road station was opened. However due to poor traffic returns, this station was closed two years later. It was not until 1879, that Cardonald Station, on the same site, was opened.

CROOKSTON STATION IN 1961.

Crookston Station, on the canal line, was opened in 1885, after the Glasgow South Western Railway had completed the line from Shields Road junction to Paisley. The link was largely built on the track of the old canal, deviating only at Cardonald Place Farm and Scott's Road, where parts of the old canal can still be seen. This view of Crookston Station, shows also the railway sidings on the right, now occupied by flats. The canal line was closed to traffic in 1982 but, following a rethink by Strathclyde Passenger Transport, was re-opened in 1989, on a single line basis. Crookston Station, which is a listed building, was partially destroyed by fire during the time the line was closed.

CORKERHILL STATION IN 1953.

Following the completion of building of engine sheds by the Glasgow & South Western Railway in 1896 at Corkerhill, a station of the same name was opened in 1897 for the use of men employed there. It never appeared on the G & SW public timetables and only came to be used by the general public from about 1920, when the Mosspark housing scheme was built. This view shows the station with a steam train approaching from Glasgow. The Corkerhill railway cottages are at the right.

MOSSPARK WEST STATION IN 1953.

With the increase in potential customers from the new houses built by the Western Heritable Company in Cardonald, the railway authorities decided to open a new station at Dundee Drive in 1934, naming it Mosspark West. As the station is some distance from Mosspark, perhaps it would have been more appropriate to have called it Cardonald South Station.

BARR'S GARAGE IN 1935.

Cardonald Smithy stood on this site in 1858, and it is now occupied by a Shell filling station ... almost 150 years of service to transport! Mrs Barr ran the post office on the right.

TRAMCAR AT CROOKSTON TERMINUS IN c1954.

The horse trams on the Paisley Road originally terminated at Copland Road, and later at the Halfway, but after the electrification in 1903, the route was extended to Hawkhead Road, where it linked with the Paisley tramway system. After 1923, when the Paisley Tramway Company was taken over by Glasgow Corporation, it was possible to travel from Elderslie to Airdrie without changing cars. The trams survived on the Paisley Road until 1962.

TRAMCAR AT VOGUE CINEMA IN 1954.

One of the hazards of the tram was that passengers had to move into the middle of the road in order to board. Here we have a no. 21 tram car at Tweedsmuir Road heading for the city. Note that Aldwych Cinema has changed its name to Vogue.

TENNIS COURTS AND BOWLING GREEN, CARDONALD

SPORTING CARDONALD c1926.

Looking from Forfar Avenue Cardonald Tennis Club is in the foreground, the Bowling Club behind and beyond that the football pitches.

Cardonald Bowling Green.

CARDONALD BOWLING CLUB IN 1914.

This original clubhouse has been altered and extended twice, and a second green was added in 1925, opened by Lady Lobnitz of Rosshall.

CARDONALD TENNIS CLUB, FORFAR AVENUE c1925.

The club opened in the early 1920s and closed in 1970, due to falling membership and high rates. The site was bought by the Corporation for housebuilding.

Tennis was first played in Cardonald in 1914 when Crookston Tennis Club opened in Carlton Gardens (now Crookston Avenue). This club closed in 1939 and in 1946 the facilities, with the adjoining hockey pitches, were taken over by the Rolls Royce Sports Club. Houses now occupy this site.

CARDONALD SHOPS.

The row of shops illustrated were among the first to serve the Cardonald district, apart from those shops at the Halfway.

As the photographs show there are shops for nearly every requirement, from a chemist to a bank - both of which are still there.

The newsagent is displaying boards announcing that John Brown's had received an order for a second Cunarder, which became the "Queen Elizabeth". This dates the photographs as being 1936.

Lacey's was a high class confectioners, particularly memorable for their wonderful chocolates.

PAISLEY PROVIDENT CO-OPERATIVE SHOP IN 1932.

The shop was built in 1924 and was the main grocers shop in Cardonald for many years. It is now a shoe shop and the adjoining house has been converted into more shops - a butchers, a hairdressers, an ironmongers and a Chinese take-away.

MACDONALD'S CAFE IN 1928.

MacDonald's Cafe was owned by the local coal merchant and over the years was a favourite meeting place. The building was extended eastwards to include other shops. Since 1969, it has housed the local Trustee Savings Bank and a laundrette.

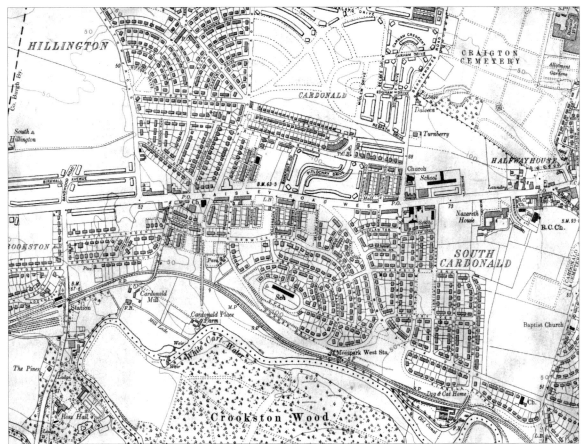

CARDONALD IN 1936 (Ordnance Survey).

DOG AND CAT HOME .

The present Cat and Dog Home opened in 1909, on a site adjacent to the Paisley Canal Railway Line, near Corkerhill Road. Prior to this date the home was situated in the grounds of Craigton House.

HILLINGTON PARK CIRCUS.

These terraced houses were among the first residential housing built in Cardonald. They were completed about 1885 and originally had a commanding view over a wide area.

HATTON GARDENS BUNGALOWS.

These semi-detached bungalows in Hatton Gardens were typical of the type of house built in Cardonald in the 1920s. These particular bungalows were sold in 1927, for the princely sum of £825 each, by a speculative builder named Lindsay, who also built the villas on the south side of the road.

WESTERN HERITABLE HOUSES.

In 1931 there was a great upsurge in housebuilding in South Cardonald and Hillington. The Western Heritable Company built the houses and offered them for rent. They were in the main "four in the block" villas, with a strong south of England flavour. By the 1950s these houses were coming on the market for sale at £750.

WESTWAY CINEMA.

Built in 1934, the Westway is the only cinema which survives in Cardonald. It could seat 1400 people, but still on many evenings, hundreds of people would be queuing outside for the second house. The cinema eventually closed in 1959 and became the Flamingo dance hall and in 1966, a bingo hall.

The WESTWAY

PAISLEY ROAD WEST
(NEAR BERRYKNOWES ROAD)

CARDONALD
Tel. No. IBROX 1458.

DAILY FROM   -   -   2.30 *p.m.*

ALWAYS A GOOD PROGRAMME
IN A CONGENIAL ATMOSPHERE

ADMISSION:— **BALCONY** 9d. and 1/-.   **STALLS** 6d.

SATURDAY:— **BALCONY** 1/-.   **STALLS** 6d. and 9d.

REDUCED PRICES till 4.30.   Stalls 4d.   Balcony 6d.

FREE PARKING AVAILABLE FOR PATRONS' MOTOR CARS

WESTWAY CINEMA ADVERT 1936.

MOSSPARK CINEMA.

This, the first cinema in the area was built in 1924 on the Paisley Road, opposite Barfillan Drive. When the Westway and the Aldwych cinemas opened in the 30s, the Mosspark tended to be looked on as slightly inferior by way of comfort, but strange to say the "Mossy", as it was affectionately known survived the other two, and showed films till 1975 when it was demolished to be replaced by a new Department of Social Security office.

ALDWYCH CINEMA, 1939.

This photograph should bring back some happy memories of evenings at the pictures. The Aldwych was the last cinema to be built in Cardonald and opened in 1938. The first film shown was "The Adventures of Robin Hood" starring Errol Flynn and Olivia de Havilland, and in colour as well. The Aldwych changed its name to the "Vogue" after the war, but eventually lost the battle to television and closed in 1964. Safeway supermarket now stands on the site.

30TH GLASGOW SCOUT HALL, LAMMERMOOR AVENUE c1933.

The 30th Scout Group started in 1909 with their headquarters in a small building north of Wedderlea Drive. By 1926, with the increasing numbers, a new H.Q. had become necessary. The scout leader at that time was Mr. Alexander Lochhead senior, the local schoolmaster. After a fund raising campaign, four old Highland Railway carriages were purchased for £36. Two carriages were erected on either side of a central hall, and roofed over. The construction was unique, as each carriage compartment allowed each patrol a den. In 1974 the hall was destroyed by fire, caused by vandalism. After an energetic fund raising effort, a new hall was completed in 1977, with the opening ceremony carried out by Mr. Bruce Millan M.P., then Secretary of State for Scotland.

CARDONALD SCHOOL CHILDREN.

Many school photographs have been taken over the years in schools everywhere. This particular one has no specific significance, but shows a typical group of Cardonald school children in 1933, putting on their best face for the photographer. Where are they now?

MOULIN ROAD AIR RAID WARDENS IN 1945.

Most of these men have passed on, except the young man on the front right, who was the messenger. The only bomb dropped in Cardonald was during the Clydebank blitz in March 1941, falling on soft ground between the Cardonald Mill and the White Cart.

HOME GUARD IN 1940.

The Home Guard was raised after the Dunkirk evacuation in 1940. This group belong to 11th City of Glasgow Battalion and the photograph was taken in front of the old 30th Glasgow Scout Hall which the Home Guard used as their headquarters.

FURTHER READING

S. Clark: Paisley - a history, 1988.

G. Crawford, W. Semple: History of the Shire of Renfrew. 1782.

Lady Elizabeth Cust: Stuarts of Aubigny. 1891.

Dr. J.B. Forsyth: Cardonald Parish Church, The First Hundred Years 1889-1989. 1989.

Glasgow Archaelogical Society Transactions Vol. XII.

Robert Guy. Crookston Castle. 1909.

William Hamilton of Wishaw: Descriptions of the Sheriffdoms of Lanark and Renfrew. c1710.

History of the Mission of Our Lady of Lourdes. 1972.

A. Kempsell: The Golden Thread, 1964.

J. Cameron Lees: The Abbey of Paisley. 1878.

A. Lindsay, Canals of Scotland, 1968.

Alexander Lochead Jnr.: First 60 years 30th Glasgow Scout Group. 1969.

Maxwell of Pollock Charters.

C.A. Oakley: The last Tram, 1962.

E.A. Pratt: Scottish Canals and Waterways. 1922.

Scots Magazine: Castles of Glasgow. 1979.

Sir James Balfour Paul. 1905. Scots Peerage.

David Semple: The Tree of Crookston, 1876.

W. Douglas Simpson: Crookston Castle. 1953.

Stephenson Locomotive Society: Caledonian Railway Centenary. 1947.

Stephenson Locomotive Society: History of the Glasgow and South Western Railway. 1950.